The Art of Travel

The Art of Travel

Amit Singh, CEO,
Manisha Holidays

Available on amazonkindle

Worldwide Published by

Pendown Press
PREMIUM BUSINESS PUBLISHER

PENDOWN PRESS LLP
An ISO 9001 & ISO 14001 Certified Co.,
Regd. Office: 3767A, Kanhaiya Nagar,
Tri Nagar, Delhi-110035
Ph.: 8130886000, 9650072927
E-mail: info@pendownpress.com
Branch Office: 1A/2A, 20, Hari Sadan, Ansari Road,
Daryaganj, New Delhi-110002
Ph.: 011-45794768
Website: PendownPress.com

Edition: 2026
Price: ₹ 399
ISBN: 978-93-7217-911-8

Layout and Cover Designed by Pendown Graphics Team

Dedicated to every family that believed in us,

that trusted us with their holidays, emotions, and expectations.

To the little joys, big smiles, and shared stories that made it all worthwhile.

With folded hands, thank you for making Manisha Holidays a part of your memories.

Table of Contents

Preface

Some people travel for fun.

Some to escape.

Some to find peace.

And some just want a break from their daily routine.

But ask any Indian family, and they'll tell you planning a trip isn't always fun. There are too many opinions, too many "what ifs," and always one person handling it all. I've seen it for years. I've felt it myself.

This book was never meant to be a book. It started with stories. Real ones. From families I've helped. From moments I've witnessed. From calls I've taken at midnight to calm a worried parent or to make sure an elderly guest finds warm food after a long journey.

Slowly, those moments started to mean something more.

Because travel isn't about big destinations. It's about how you feel when you're away, and when you come back.

If you're reading this, I just want to say thank you. Thank you for giving me your time, your trust, and your eyes on these words. I don't have fancy English or big travel terms to throw at you. Just some lived experiences, small truths, and maybe a smile or two.

Read this as if a friend is talking to you.

And when you plan your next trip, I hope a small part of this book walks with you.

Warmly,

Amit Singh

Acknowledgements

Every step I've taken, every milestone I've crossed, has been possible because of the people who stood by me quietly, constantly, and unconditionally.

To my parents: If today I have wings, it's only because you gave them to me. Your values, trust, and silent guidance shaped the person I am. You believed in me even when I doubted myself, and that belief became my strength. You taught me to live with honesty, to give without expecting, and to walk with courage.

To my wife: You've been my steady hand through storms and successes alike. The way you've balanced home and supported me with wisdom and grace is something I deeply admire. Thank you for being my strongest support system.

To my kids: You light up my world. Your laughter, love, and presence inspire me to be better every single day.

To all my mentors: Your wisdom has been a lighthouse in my business journey. I'm forever grateful for your guidance and time.

To my incredible team at Manisha Holidays: You've been the foundation behind every big and small achievement. Your energy, creativity, and dedication mean the world to me.

To our clients: Thank you for your trust, your feedback, and your constant inspiration. You are a vital part of this journey.

Special thanks to **Dinesh Verma and the amazing Pendown Press team.** This book wouldn't have seen the light of day without your effort and encouragement.

And finally, to all friends, family, and well-wishers: Your presence in my life is my blessing. Even if I haven't named you here, you remain in my heart.

This journey is ours. Thank you for walking it with me.

Why This Book

- Because Google can't calm a crying toddler on a road trip.
- Because planning a family holiday shouldn't feel like a math exam.
- Because everyone from Nani to niece deserves a moment of joy.
- Because you shouldn't have to choose between peace and planning.
- Because behind every perfect photo is someone sweating over details.
- Because memories matter more than mileage.
- Because you don't need 50 locations, just the right five.
- Because travel agents aren't just agents; they're emotion managers.
- Because one good trip can bring a whole family closer.
- Because this isn't just a book.

It's a friend who knows the way.

Introduction: The Journey Within

"I used to think planning a holiday meant picking a place, booking a hotel, and packing your bags. Simple, right? But travel, true travel, isn't just about going somewhere. It's about becoming someone else for a few days. It's about surrendering to a new rhythm, understanding different cultures, and uncovering stories not found in guidebooks."

~ Amit Singh

When I started this business nearly two decades ago, I was a different man. My world revolved around simple itineraries and spreadsheets. If someone said Kerala, I'd imagine houseboats. If someone said Goa, I'd list beaches and shacks. Back then, travel was a transaction. Today, I know it's transformation.

Over the years, I've met hundreds of travellers: young couples, retired explorers, excited families, first-time fliers, solo dreamers. They all came to me with the same destination on paper but wildly different dreams in their hearts.

Take Kerala, for instance:

One family might visit for three days of houseboating bliss, drifting lazily over backwaters. Another couple might stay eight nights, seeking the echo of wildlife in Thekkady or the healing touch of a monsoon-soaked spa.

Same destination, different desires.

That's when I truly understood: **Travel is not about the place; it's about the purpose.**

Travel Isn't One Size Fits All

In my experience, there are no fixed packages, only personal journeys.

- A young couple on a honeymoon needs privacy, romance, and quiet luxury.
- A family seeks safety, variety, and comfort for their kids.
- A group of college friends wants thrills, affordability, and nightlife.
- A corporate team demands precision, timing, and structure.

And what about comparison?

Today, everyone has a WhatsApp-forwarded itinerary, a cousin who booked a cheaper trip, or a brand-name portal promising deals. But here's what people don't realize:

You can't compare just the price.

You must compare the support, the intention, and the human touch.

Because once your payment is done, what you truly carry with you is trust, not tickets.

What We Offer (And Why It Matters)

At **Manisha Holidays,** I built a system that values customisation over convenience. I ask each customer one simple question:

"What's your intention for this trip?"

Because only when we understand your why, can we design your how.

And trust me, things do go wrong. Flights get delayed. Cabs break down. Hotels forget room service policies. That's the truth most travel companies won't admit up front. But I do. Because we aren't perfect, and neither is the world. But we are present.

If something goes wrong, I don't calculate losses; I resolve issues.

If needed, I change hotels, upgrade stays, make calls, and spend late nights without counting rupees or refunds.

Because I don't measure success in bookings, I measure it in memories.

A Note on Loyalty & Lessons

Let me share a story that still makes me smile.

One of my long-time clients, **Dr. Ranjan Mohan Sharma,** recommended us to his friends from Jaipur, **Mr. Ashish Rana and Ms. Priyanka Jain.** I crafted a Singapore package for both families. While Dr. Sharma was ready to go with us, the Jaipur family was hesitant, loyal to their own agent.

They decided to compare.

Both agents submitted packages. Ours won not only on price, but also on **clarity, inclusions, and care.**

But what followed surprised me more.

Ms. Priyanka Jain had so many questions, at times five calls a day!

And with every query, she made me think deeper. Her detailed concerns, though challenging, became my blueprint for improving every future package. Today, I thank her not just as a client but as a teacher. And her referrals from Jaipur? They've become a network of trust we cherish deeply.

I will cover the whole story in one of the upcoming chapters. And let me tell you, this is just the trailer, as the saying goes: '*Picture abhi baaki hai mere dost!*'

In this book, I will not sell you destinations.

I will share with you the **philosophy behind travel, the art of empathy, the importance of intention, and the lessons learned from mishaps and miracles.**

Because **"The Art of Travel"** is not about where you go.

It's about who you become on the way.

CHAPTER 1

THE BIRTH OF MANISHA HOLIDAYS

"It didn't begin with a bang... it began with a budget and a belief."

To be honest, I never dreamed of becoming a travel company owner.

Back in the day, I was just like everyone else, working, earning, and planning the occasional family holiday like a checklist:

- Destination
- Hotel
- Sightseeing
- Done.

But over time, I started noticing something strange.

People around me were going to the same places but having very different experiences. Some came back smiling ear to ear, while others came back with long faces and longer complaints.

And then it hit me: **it's not the destination, it's the design.**

You can go to Switzerland and still have a boring time if it's not planned right. Or you can go to Himachal and feel like royalty if it's curated properly.

That thought stayed with me.

From Planning for Friends to Planning as a Profession

I started helping friends and relatives with their holidays.

One would say, *"Bhaiya, you've been to Goa. Book karwa do na."*

Another would say, "Amit, you know Thailand well, can you guide us?"

Slowly, my evenings were full of calls, bookings, advice, and "*kitna ka padega*" type questions.

One day, my wife looked at me and said,

"*You're doing this full time without a salary. Might as well start a company!*"

And just like that, **Manisha Holidays was born.**

(Yes, named after her. Smart men know how to keep their wives happy, right?)

No Office, No Staff... Just One Phone and a Lot of Hope

In the beginning, there was no office, no big banners, no staff.

Just one notebook, one basic mobile phone, and one big dream.

I used to run around meeting hotel vendors, calling cab drivers, following up with clients, and basically doing jugaad at every step.

Sometimes, I felt like a magician, *juggling* dates, flights, visas, and temper tantrums all at once.

I still remember once I was explaining an entire trip to a client while standing in a long ATM line. **Multitasking was my middle name!**

First Clients, First Mistakes, First Lessons

My first official client came through a friend's friend.

The budget was tight, the expectations were sky-high, and my experience was zero.

But I gave it my best.

I made a few mistakes, learned a lot more, and somehow managed to pull it off.

When the trip ended, the client said, "Amit bhai, you handled it better than any big brand."

That day, I didn't earn much money, but I earned something far more valuable: confidence.

Word of Mouth: The Best Advertising

In today's world of Facebook ads and Google keywords, I still believe nothing beats word of mouth.

One happy client tells three people, and boom, you've got a mini fan club.

That's how *Manisha Holidays grew.*

No big ad budgets, no celebrity endorsements, just real experiences and real relationships.

From one room in my house to an actual office,

From ten queries a month to hundreds,

From managing trips to managing a whole team,

It's been a long journey, full of bumps, turns, and beautiful views.

What I Learned Early On

- ❖ People don't just want tickets, they want trust.
- ❖ You don't need to know everything, just be ready to learn.
- ❖ Clients remember how you made them feel more than what you booked.
- ❖ And if you ever mess up, own it, fix it, and move on.

Because travel is not just a service.

It's a feeling.

And every good holiday becomes a story if done right.

"People will forget what you said, people will forget what you did, but people will never forget how you made them feel."

~ Maya Angelou

CHAPTER 2

Same Destination, Different Desires

"It's not just where you go, it's why you go."

In my early days, I used to think, "Kerala means houseboats."

Simple, right?

Backwaters, banana chips, and a boat ride.

But oh boy, I was wrong. So wrong.

Because one day, a client called me and said,

"Amit ji, I want to explore the wild side of Kerala — jungles, safaris, and raw nature."

I was like, "Wait... not houseboats?"

And then another couple came to me and said,

"We want to go to Kerala in the monsoon. Spa, luxury, green views — we just want to relax."

I thought, "Aren't houseboats the main thing?"

Turns out, not everyone's **Kerala is the same.**

One State, Many Stories

This is when I realised that destinations don't change, but intentions do.

Let's say five people are going to Goa:

- One wants beaches and beer.
- One wants churches and forts.

- One wants flea markets and shopping.
- One wants peace and yoga.
- One just wants photos for Instagram.

Same place, five totally different holidays.

So, What's the Trick?

Here's the trick: **Before you plan the trip, understand the traveller.**

That's why, at Manisha Holidays, we don't start with "Where do you want to go?"

We start with **"Why do you want to go?"**

Because:

- A honeymoon couple doesn't want the same experience as a school group.
- A joint family has very different needs from a solo traveller.
- A group of friends on a budget trip will think very differently from a couple celebrating their silver jubilee.

In fact, sometimes the same person behaves differently at different places.

I have seen clients spend ₹80,000 per night in the Maldives but go for a ₹2,000 hotel in Rishikesh.

Why?

Because every destination has its own mood, and so do we.

Questions That Matter

We ask questions like:

- "What's your idea of a perfect holiday?"
- "Do you prefer lazy mornings or packed schedules?"

- "Are you a beach baby or a mountain lover?"
- "Foodie or fitness freak?"
- "Room service or street food?"

Because once we know you, we can plan your version of the holiday, not just the brochure one.

Real People, Real Needs

Let me break it down:

Traveller Type	What They Want
Young Couple	Privacy, romance, candlelight dinners
Family with Kids	Safety, entertainment, kid-friendly hotels
Group of Friends	Flexibility, nightlife, fun activities
Corporate Group	Comfort, timing, smooth execution
Spiritual Seeker	Peace, purpose, guided visits

And here's the funniest part:

Even if the location is exactly the same, their needs will still be poles apart.

Lesson for Every Traveller

So here's my advice:

Never go on a holiday blindly.

Don't just book flights and hotels and assume everything will magically fall into place.

Travel isn't a pizza you order; it's a full-course meal.

You need to know the ingredients, the spice level, and the chef! 🧑‍🍳

And don't just compare prices.

Compare what's inside the package.

- ❖ What are you getting?
- ❖ How much are you saving, not just in money but in headache?

Some big companies may give you a robotic reply at midnight.

We give you **Amit Singh** or **Manisha Singh** on the phone, even at 2 AM if needed.

Because with us, you don't just get a trip.

You get a team that truly cares.

"Travel isn't always pretty. It isn't always comfortable. But that's okay. The journey changes you; it should change you."

~ Anthony Bourdain

And that's what we believe in: travel that transforms.

CHAPTER 3

COMPARISON IS A TRAP

> *"Don't compare apples to oranges, especially if one is rotten inside."*

Let me tell you the truth.

One of the most common things people do before booking a holiday is:

"*Let me check if another travel agent is giving this cheaper.*"

And honestly?

That's fine. In fact, smart travellers should compare.

But the problem is most people compare the wrong things.

Price vs Value

Here's how most people compare:

"Package A is ₹5,000 cheaper than Package B. Let's go with A."

But here's what they often miss:

- Is the package putting you in a poorly located hotel?
- Is it giving you only one sightseeing trip instead of three?
- Does it include breakfast, airport transfers, GST?
- And most importantly, what happens if something goes wrong?

Let me say it loud and clear:

Price is visible. Value is hidden.

Bot vs Buddy

Let's talk about customer support.

Many "big brands" offer 24x7 customer care, but guess what?

It's usually a calling bot.

Press 1 for this, press 2 for that...

And by the time you finally reach a human, your holiday is already over.

At Manisha Holidays, **you don't press numbers. You dial a name.**

We personally talk to you, sometimes even when we're on our own holiday.

That's the level of dedication we bring.

Real-Life Litmus Test

Let me share an example.

A family once asked me:

"Amit bhai, your Singapore package is ₹3,000 more than another agent's. Why should we go with you?"

I smiled and said, "Let's play a small game. Ask both of us the same set of questions. Let's see who answers everything and helps you genuinely."

By the end of the day, the other agent had replied to just two WhatsApp messages.

I, on the other hand, had sent them:

- A personalised voice note
- A customised itinerary
- A list of restaurants near their hotel
- And even live weather updates for their travel dates

The next day, I got a message:

"Sir, we are going ahead with you. Money can be saved again; time and trust can't."

One Call Can Save a Trip

Most travellers don't realise that things can go wrong on a trip.

And when they do, who you call decides whether your trip is saved or sunk.

Flight delayed? Hotel issue? The cab didn't come?

Ask yourself: Will your ₹500-cheaper agent pick up the phone at 11 PM?

I will.

Because for me, it's not just a package; it's your memory, and **I treat it with the care it truly deserves.**

Don't Be Penny Wise, Trip Foolish

Let me tell you one of my favourite idioms:

"Cheap is expensive if it ruins your peace."

A ₹300-cheaper room with no AC in peak summer?

A ₹1,000-saved hotel that smells like a pickle factory?

Is that worth it?

Absolutely not.

Your holiday should not become a regret.

"Price is what you pay. Value is what you get."

~ Warren Buffett

Because great deals don't just save money; they protect your peace of mind.

What to Actually Compare:

Instead of comparing...	Try comparing...
Just the price	Hotel names, inclusions, refund policy
Itinerary names	Time spent per place, travel gaps
Big brand logos	Actual reviews, real human support
Discounts	Hidden costs, fine print, emergency help

So, the next time someone tells you:

"I got this deal ₹2,000 cheaper..."

Just smile and say:

"Did you check what's inside the box?"

CHAPTER 4

Every Trip Teaches Me Something

"Sometimes you travel to see the world. Sometimes, the world travels through your experiences."

Let me tell you something straight from the heart: **no trip is ever truly perfect.**

And that's not because we don't try, but because **life has its own plans.**

Despite all the care, coordination, and confirmations, there will always be a surprise or two.

But here's the beautiful part:

Every trip I've planned has taught me something new.

Sometimes I learn from the client, sometimes from the situation, and sometimes just from a good old-fashioned mess-up!

Let me share two stories with you.

Story 1: Jaipur vs Singapore

Dr. Ranjan Mohan Sharma has been one of my oldest clients, someone who trusts me blindly. One day, he called and said:

"Amit bhai, my friend Mr. Ashish Rana and his wife Priyanka Jain from Jaipur want to go to Singapore. Please plan a nice package for both families."

Done!

With full heart, I created a complete plan: flights, hotel, sightseeing, meals, all inclusive.

But here comes the twist: Mr. Rana's family already had a regular agent they always used for travel. They didn't want to leave him.

So they asked Dr. Sharma, "Let's just compare Amit's plan with our usual agent's and then decide."

Dr. Sharma, being a gentleman, said, "Let's compare and then choose the best."

Fair game!

Now here comes Ms. Priyanka Jain. She had so many questions that she called me five times a day. Some agents might find that annoying, but not me.

In fact, every time she asked something new, I learned how to:

- ❖ Explain complex visa steps in simpler terms
- ❖ Create short, to-the-point itineraries
- ❖ Add Indian meal options in Singapore
- ❖ Offer hotel comparisons with visuals for easier decisions

Her questions were not doubts; they were training modules for me!

And guess what?

They booked through me, and after returning, she gave me regular business from Jaipur.

Today, she's not just a happy client; she's a walking, talking ad for Manisha Holidays.

Story 2: Thailand Tangle

One day I got a call from two stags from Haldwani, regular Thailand travellers.

They said, *"Amit bhai, we want a quick five-day trip to Pattaya. We already have a hotel in mind."*

"Okay," I said. "I'll design the package as per your choice."

Everything was booked. They landed. And then… chaos.

They said:

"Yeh kya hotel hai, bhai? This is not the one we wanted!"

I was confused.

"But sir, this is exactly what you asked me to book."

"Yes, but we thought you'd booked the other branch. This one is terrible!"

Now here comes the problem: the hotel was non-refundable. I couldn't cancel it.

But instead of arguing and wasting time, I acted. I immediately booked another hotel (the correct one) for them from my own pocket.

Yes, it was a small loss, but it became a big gain in trust.

Today, they've sent me over six referrals. And every time they call, they start with,

"Bhai, ab toh bas aap hi ho."

The Lesson

Every single holiday teaches me a little more about:

- ❖ People's psychology
- ❖ What comfort really means
- ❖ How to manage expectations
- ❖ How to be ready for the unexpected

Some people want luxury with simplicity.

Some want budget with class.

Some want photos more than experiences.

And some just want peace, far from any crowd.

But here's something I deeply believe now:

A holiday is not just about going outside, eating good food, or clicking photos.

A holiday is a bond.

A holiday is an energy refill.

A holiday is a memory bank.

Whether it's a short break with friends, a long family vacation, or a small trip with your spouse, it's an investment in relationships.

When you look back at your life, what moments make you smile the most?

Not that random Tuesday in the office.

Not that client call.

But that sunset at the beach, that laugh with your kids, that late-night tea on a hill station.

I've seen it again and again: holidays refresh your soul and energise your mind.

And once you're back, your focus at work is sharper, your stress level is lower, and your heart is fuller.

From College to Career: My First Holiday Plan

When I was still studying, yes, young, confused, and hopeful, I once got the opportunity to plan a holiday for my classmates and teachers.

Destination? Nainital.

The twist? I had absolutely no clue about Nainital. I didn't know the route, the hotels, or anything else. But I said, "*Chalo kar ke dekhte hain.*" I planned that trip. I managed that trip. And honestly, to my surprise, it went great. People had fun. Teachers appreciated it. Students remembered it. And I think that's when this journey started. That was the seed, the beginning of what became my full-time passion, and today, my profession.

So yes, every trip teaches me something. But the biggest lesson? If travel is done right, it becomes a story that lives forever.

Or as Mark Twain beautifully said:

"Twenty years from now, you will be more disappointed by the things you didn't do than by the ones you did. So throw off the bowlines. Sail away from the safe harbor."

That college trip to Nainital was my boat. And I'm still sailing, with purpose, with people, and with stories that continue to unfold.

CHAPTER 5

Holiday Planning is Not Like Grocery Shopping!

Let's be honest; planning a holiday isn't like picking up bread, butter, and bhindi from the supermarket.

You can't just say,

"Bhaiya, ek Shimla pack kar do... aur side mein thoda adventure bhi daal dena."

Holiday planning takes thought.

It needs time, energy, and, most importantly, someone who gets you.

Because you're not buying vegetables; you're building memories—memories that will live in photo frames, phone galleries, and family conversations for years. You want it to feel special, seamless, and soulful.

Why Cheap Isn't Always Cheerful

Let's be honest, we all love discounts. Who doesn't like saving a few bucks?

But when it comes to holidays, "sasta" can sometimes turn into "suffer."

That low-cost hotel might have no windows.

That budget cab might cancel at the last minute.

That too-good-to-be-true package might come with a hundred hidden conditions.

In the end, you didn't save money. You just paid in stress.

Cheap Plans = Expensive Regrets.

The Role of the Right Travel Agent

A good travel agent is like a good tailor.

They stitch your holiday just the way it fits you.

Not too tight, not too loose. Not over the top. Just perfect.

A good agent doesn't just ask, "Where do you want to go?" They ask:

- ❖ Who's travelling? Kids? Elders? Both?
- ❖ What's your vibe: adventure, relaxation, sightseeing?
- ❖ How much time do you have?

They won't throw you on a 12-hour bus ride just because the hotel is cheaper there.

They'll suggest options that make your trip smooth, not shaky.

True Story: The "Grocery Basket" Traveller

A client once came to us with a full-on mix-match holiday wishlist:

"Bhaiya, I want 5-star hotel ka comfort, budget room ka rate, mountains ka view, beach ka sunset, and a full Delhi–Manali–Goa–Kerala–Andaman trip in 5 days."

It was like asking for pizza with rajma chawal on top. 😄

We smiled, took a deep breath, then gently explained the reality vs fantasy part.

Instead of that mad race across states, we reworked the plan into something meaningful:

A simple 3-night stay in Munnar with their kids.

No running around. No airport hopping.

Just clean air, lush views, and quality time.

And guess what?

They came back glowing.

Later, they called and said,

"Thanks for not letting us go with our original plan. We actually relaxed for once!"

Sometimes, less is more.

What We've Learned

Holiday planning is a skill.

It's not about throwing random places into a bag and shaking it.

It's about:

- ❖ Understanding the traveller
- ❖ Matching comfort with budget
- ❖ Keeping a balance of rest and fun
- ❖ Always having a **Plan B** when **Plan A** decides to misbehave

That's why a good planner is not just a "booking person."

They're part psychologist, part magician, and a full-time problem solver.

"The difference between ordinary and extraordinary is that little extra."

~ Jimmy Johnson

And in travel, that "little extra" often makes the biggest difference, not just in your trip, but in your memories.

CHAPTER 6

UNCLE'S LIST VS. KID'S DREAM VS BUDGET – FINDING THE BALANCE

Every family trip starts with one big plan.

And then it quickly turns into **five opinions, seven suggestions, and a group chat full of confusion.** 😅

Let's break it down.

Uncle want temples and museums

He's already made a list:

- Famous mandir ✔
- Local history museum ✔
- Early morning walks ✔
- No loud music ✖
- Back in hotel by 6 PM ✔

He even printed out Wikipedia pages. Yes, printed.

Kids want waterparks and burgers

They have their own wishlist:

- Pool ✔
- Slides ✔
- Ice cream ✔
- Zero lectures ✔
- Unlimited cartoons ✔

They don't care if they're in Manali or Mumbai, as long as there's fun, they're on board. History? Meh. Heritage? Maybe.

But waterpark? **YES, PLEASE.**

Budget says, "Please control!"

The wallet, however, has its own story:

- Can't afford 5-star luxury
- Flight + Hotel + Sightseeing = Headache
- "Dekho, trip toh karni hai… par EMI chalu hai."

So now you're stuck between Uncle's **itinerary,** the kids' **imagination,** and your budget's **limitations.**

So what do you do?

Finding Middle Ground

This is where smart planning comes in.

Instead of a packed, stressful trip that tries to please everyone 100%...

we suggest a balanced mix:

- ❖ Let Uncle have his morning aarti and heritage stroll.
- ❖ Let the kids jump into the hotel pool in the afternoon.
- ❖ Let the budget chill, because everything's pre-planned and paid smartly.

Truth is, nobody needs everything.

They just need something of their own to enjoy.

Even a simple chai break on a hillside makes everyone smile if you're relaxed.

How We Handle Family Drama (Softly)

When families come to us, it's not just travel planning, it's emotional management!

We patiently listen to:

- ❖ Daddy's "yeh jagah toh zaroor jaana hai"
- ❖ Mummy's "thoda shopping bhi karna hai"
- ❖ Kids' "only pool, no rules"
- ❖ And yes, the ultimate line:

"Budget mein hi rakhna, bhaiya."

We build the trip like a thali:

a little bit of everything, taste, variety, satisfaction.

No one leaves hungry or cranky. Everyone goes home with a happy story.

Real Example – The "Jiju, Baby, and Budget" Case

A family once came to us with a classic trio of challenges:

- Jiju wanted trekking.
- The baby needed nap time.
- And Nani wanted darshan at every stop.

Challenge?

Only 4 days and a tight budget.

Solution?

We planned an easy stay in Rishikesh with:

- One adventure day for Jiju.
- A peaceful riverbank hotel for Nani.
- Baby-friendly spots with enough downtime.
- And an evening Ganga Aarti for everyone to enjoy together.

They returned with photos, smiles, and no complaints.

Now that's a win in our book!

The Bottom Line

You don't need 50 locations.

You just need a few good moments with your people.

Let Uncle click his temple selfie.

Let the kids make a splash.

Let the wallet breathe.

And most importantly, **let yourself relax, because that's what a holiday is for.**

CHAPTER 7

Handle With Care: Why Senior Citizens and Babies Need Special Planning

Let's face it: **planning a trip with toddlers and grandpas is a different sport altogether.**

This isn't a backpacking adventure.

It's not a college road trip.

And it's definitely not an army camp.

You can't do 8 places in one day.

You can't say, "We'll manage."

Because the moment you say that,

someone will either say "Mujhe chakkar aa raha hai..."

or someone will start crying. And trust me, it's not always the baby. 😅

Babies – Cute but High Maintenance

Here's the baby travel starter pack:

- Milk timings
- Diaper changes
- Nap schedule
- Temperature sensitivity
- Sudden meltdowns (without warning!)

And then comes the ask:

"Please arrange fresh cow milk for my baby."

Not tetra pack, not powdered, gai ka doodh hona chahiye. Fresh. Twice a day.

You say okay, and before you know it,

"Hope you've also arranged for a babysitter?" 😅

No kidding. We've actually heard this.

So yes, when you're travelling with a tiny human, we always suggest:

- Short travel distances
- Comfortable, clean hotel rooms
- Baby-friendly food
- Microwave access for warm meals
- Cow milk (if possible!)
- And backup plans (for the backup plans)

We always tell parents:

A calm baby = a calm holiday.

So let's carry the stroller and the soft toy, and leave the stress behind.

Nana-Nani – Deserve Extra Comfort

Senior citizens aren't looking for DJ nights or ziplining.

They want:

- Good sleep
- Less walking
- Nice weather
- Basic comfort
- Spiritual vibes, if possible

Also, many have:

- Blood pressure tablets
- Knee issues
- Diet restrictions
- And that one "tel ki botal" they won't travel without

So we pick places with:

- Lifts, not just stairs
- Clean bathrooms and good lighting

- Early dinner options
- Less running around

And believe us, if Nana-Nani are happy, **the whole trip becomes peaceful.**

Our Job: Making It All Work

We're not just booking rooms; we're booking peace of mind.

We make sure:

- The car doesn't shake too much
- The hotel staff provides warm water when requested
- The driver is patient (and doesn't play Yo Yo Honey Singh at full volume 😅)
- The food is neither too spicy nor too bland, just thik-thak

We even remind families to carry shawls, snacks, and charger wires because no one wants to hunt for baby wipes at midnight in a new city.

Real Example – The "3-Generation Trip"

One family once planned a trip with:

- A 2-year-old
- A 68-year-old
- A stressed mom
- And an excited dad

They wanted to go to Jaipur.

What did we do?

- Booked a resort just 20 minutes from the main city (peace + access)
- Arranged a car with child seat and step stool

- Got them early check-in so the baby could nap on arrival
- Added a sunset camel ride (slow, short, senior-friendly)
- Tracked down a local dairy for fresh cow milk twice a day

Result?

Happy baby. Happy Dadi. Relaxed parents.

Everyone came back with photos and zero drama.

The Bottom Line

Trips are not just for the young and restless.

They're for everyone, but only if planned right.

With babies and elders, you can't wing it.

You plan with:

- Love, logic, and little hacks
- A slower pace
- And lots of cushion time

Because one happy baby giggle or one smile from Dadaji?

Totally worth it.

CHAPTER 8

It's the Little Things That Count

Simple Gestures That Matter

Sometimes, it's the small things that make the biggest difference. A warm cup of tea, a kind smile, or a little extra care, these are the moments guests remember most.

At Manisha Holidays, we believe that travel is not just about the places you visit but about how you feel while you're there. And often, that feeling comes from the small acts of kindness.

One rainy afternoon, a family arrived tired and wet. Without a big welcome speech or fancy gifts, we offered them hot tea and some pakoras, freshly made in our kitchen. They sat quietly, sipping and relaxing. That simple cup of tea became the memory they cherished from their trip.

We also know that every guest is different. Some like their tea strong; some prefer it light. Some want extra sugar; others, none at all. Our staff listens carefully and tries to serve it just the way guests like it.

When Small Things Become Big Relief

Once, a family was traveling with a baby. The parents didn't ask for a fancy babysitter or toys or anything expensive. They just wanted fresh cow milk for the baby every day. Simple, right?

The hotel staff looked a bit puzzled: "Cow milk? Seriously? Not chai or coffee?" But we made sure they got it, no questions asked.

And you know what? That little thing made the whole trip easier for the family. The baby was happy, the parents were relaxed, and the holiday went as smooth as butter.

That's why it's so important to tell your travel agent everything, even the small stuff that might seem unimportant. Because every family is different. Every trip is different. And every little thing counts.

So don't be shy. If you want fresh cow milk for your baby, ask for it. If you want a quiet room, a special meal, or even a wake-up call at dawn, say it loud and clear.

At the end of the day, holidays are about feeling comfortable and making great memories. And those memories start with getting the little things right. After all, it's the small sips that make the big gulp enjoyable!

Trust is built in these small moments. When guests know they can count on us for a little extra care, they feel at home, even when far away.

That's why, for us, hospitality is more than a business. It's about respect, warmth, and genuine care.

What Does This Tell You?

When you pick your travel partner, see if they care about the small stuff that matters to you. Are they willing to go the extra mile, even if it means losing a bit on the cost side?

If I were to suggest a synonym of trust and assurance that will be Manisha Holidays. One of the most promising travel agencies I came across the sense of belongingness and comfort one gets with Manisha will leave customers speechless. having a team of professional and dynamic, dedicated staff who will not only follow your instructions and wishes but will also give your ideas out of the box which can be financially very profitable for a customer and such a charm is little less when it comes to travelling agencies.

Mr Zeeshan Khan

Advocate Delhi high Court

We have been associated with Manisha Travels for the last fifteen years.

They've taken care of our domestic and international travel needs on countless occasions.

The staff is courteous, efficient and trustworthy.

We congratulate them on being such a professional unit, and hope they continue to provide services similarly in the future as well.

Dr Anupam Ahuja

The tour was really amazing and a must-visit

Dr. Vikram Gyan & Ms. Prerna Gupta

Doctor

Thanks Manisha mam for everything you did to ensure we had the best vacation in Vietnam. Excellent service, prompt responses to any queries and everything was sorted for us. We always book our holidays through this company and will continue to do so.

Mr Kamlesh Kumar & Mrs Kanida Joshi

CHAPTER 9

WOMEN IN TRAVEL – MRS. MANISHA'S LENS

A Woman's Intuition in Planning Perfect Trips

Travel planning is not just about dates, flights, or hotels; it's about understanding what people really want. And that's where a woman's intuition plays a big role.

Mrs. Manisha often says, "*Har family ka apna ek connection hota hai travel ke saath. Kisi ko relaxation chahiye, kisi ko adventure, aur kisi ko sirf apno ke saath quality time.*"

Understanding these needs even before the client explains them is what makes a trip perfect.

Sometimes it's small things, like a hotel with a quiet corner for grandparents, or a restaurant with good kids' food. "*Aisi choti choti baatein jo shayad guest bol ke na bataye, woh hum pehle hi soch lete hain.*"

This instinct helps Manisha Holidays create trips that feel personal and special, not just another booking.

Challenges and Strengths of Being a Female Travel Entrepreneur

The travel business isn't easy, and being a woman adds an extra layer of challenges. Late nights, leading teams, and handling unexpected issues on the go are all part of the job.

"Travel industry mein ek woman ka hona matlab hai double responsibility lena."

Balancing personal life and work is a constant juggle, but Mrs. Manisha believes women bring strengths that work perfectly for travel.

"*Patience, empathy, multitasking, yeh sab hum naturally karte hain.*" Whether it's calming a worried parent, negotiating with vendors, or handling last-minute itinerary changes, women's skills help smooth out rough edges.

Mrs. Manisha also talks about the power of building trust, especially with families and solo travelers who want extra care. "Women clients feel comfortable when they know a woman is handling their trip. It's not just business; it's about feeling safe and understood."

Managing Backend Operations, Client Relationships, and Design

Behind the scenes, there's a lot happening that guests don't see: booking tickets, coordinating with hotels, arranging local transport, managing payments, the list goes on.

And Mrs. Manisha oversees all of this closely.

She says, "*Har client ka experience unique hota hai, toh unke liye packages bhi personalized hone chahiye.*" It's not a one-size-fits-all deal. Every trip is designed with care and attention to detail.

Manisha Holidays is known for that personal touch, calling guests during their holiday to check if everything is fine, quickly solving any problem, and remembering special occasions. This care turns first-time customers into lifelong friends.

CHAPTER 10

Beyond Borders – International Stories

Bringing Indian Care to Faraway Places

Travel is not just about visiting new places. It is also about feeling at home, wherever you go. At Manisha Holidays, we have been helping guests explore beautiful countries like Singapore, Dubai, Bali, and the Maldives for many years. Each journey is special, not only because of the destination, but because of the care, comfort, and warmth we bring along.

Whether it is a family looking for a quiet beach, a group of friends seeking adventure, or newlyweds on their honeymoon, we make sure they feel comfortable and safe, no matter how far from home they are.

Our team knows that small things make a big difference. We arrange familiar meals for guests missing ghar ka khana, guide them patiently through unfamiliar streets, and offer support at every step, **available 24/7** even across time zones.

Hear It From Them

Here are some stories from our guests' travels abroad that show how we keep the spirit of ***Atithi Devo Bhava*** alive, wherever you go.

A Family's Peaceful Holiday in Bali

The Sharma family wanted a calm and peaceful holiday in Bali. They wanted quiet beaches, fresh air, and a place where their children could play safely. We found them a small resort close to nature, away from busy tourist spots. Our local team made sure they got home-style Indian meals.

The children enjoyed playing outside, and the parents liked walking on the beach. The family later told us, "*We felt like we were at home, even so far away.*"

Dubai: The City of Dreams and Warmth

Many guests visit Dubai for shopping and sightseeing. But for us, it is also about making the trip easy and comfortable. When Mr. and Mrs. Gupta traveled with their elderly parents, we arranged special transport, wheelchair help, and quiet hotel rooms. We also got them Indian breakfast items and booked tickets to family shows.

The Guptas said, "*Thanks to Manisha Holidays, we felt cared for all the time.*"

Singapore: The Little Big City

Singapore is popular because it is clean, safe, and full of things to see. For a group of friends on their first international trip, we arranged a city tour, local SIM cards, and clear help with public transport.

They said, "*We were nervous about traveling abroad, but your team made it easy and fun.*"

The Maldives: Love and Relaxation

Many couples choose the Maldives for its beautiful beaches. One couple wanted a special surprise for their anniversary. We arranged a private dinner on the beach with flowers and candles.

The husband wrote, "You helped us make memories we will always remember."

What We Believe

Traveling abroad can be exciting but also challenging. Language, culture, and food can be different. And sometimes, even the smallest discomfort can feel big when you are far from home. We believe every traveler deserves care that feels personal and familiar. That is why we work hard to know what each guest needs and bring the warmth of India wherever they go.

Our job is not just to book tickets or hotels but to build trust and happiness. Because wherever you travel, feeling cared for makes all the difference.

Travel is not just about going far away. It is about carrying a piece of home wherever you go.

At Manisha Holidays, we believe that even when you cross countries and oceans, the warmth of Indian care follows you.

Take our trip to Singapore. Families, couples, and groups all joined us. They wanted to see the bright city but also feel comforted by familiar kindness.

One family from Delhi told us,

"We were worried about the food and language. But Manisha Holidays made sure we had simple meals we liked, and someone who spoke Hindi was always nearby."

And that one line, that feeling of being understood, is what sets us apart.

Dubai, Bali, and the Maldives have also become favorite destinations. We have planned special trips for honeymooners, friends celebrating, and large families.

In Bali, a group of friends celebrated a birthday. We arranged a quiet dinner by the beach, with local music and home-style food. The smile on their faces said it all.

Even far away from India, guests tell us they feel at home because of small things, a warm hello, patience, and attention to detail.

Our role is not just to arrange flights and hotels. It is to bring a little piece of India with us, wherever our guests go.

This is what makes international travel with Manisha Holidays different. It is not just a trip. It is a caring journey.

CHAPTER 11

How to Set Your Holiday Budget Without Cutting Corners (With Little-Known Travel Tips)

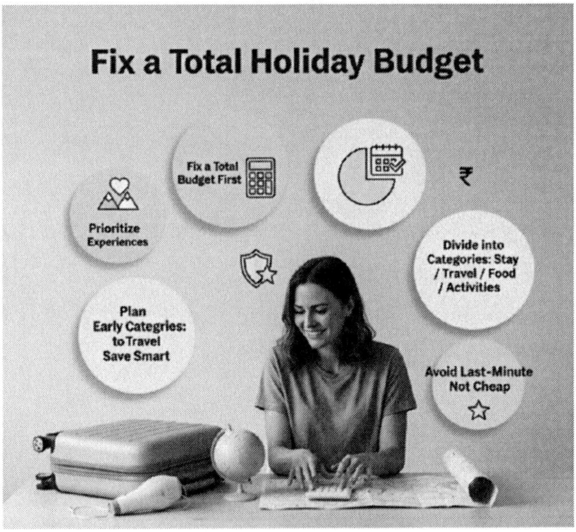

Budget is always the big question. "How much will this trip cost?" But here's the thing: setting a holiday budget is not about squeezing every rupee till it screams.

It's about making smart, thoughtful choices so you don't end up regretting it later.

1. Know What Matters to You

Start by asking yourself: *What's most important to me on this trip?*

- ❖ Is it a comfortable stay or the best hotel?
- ❖ Do you want to try local food or eat only in five-star restaurants?
- ❖ Are experiences like safaris or sightseeing must-haves?
- ❖ Will you be okay with basic transportation or need private cabs?

Once you know your priorities, it is easier to allocate money where it counts.

2. Don't Cut Corners on Essentials

Sometimes we try to save on important things and then pay for it later.

Cheap hotels might mean uncomfortable sleep or unsafe neighborhoods.

Ignoring travel insurance can lead to huge costs if something goes wrong.

So always keep some buffer for important things. It is better to spend a little more and stay worry-free.

3. Plan for Hidden Costs

Some costs sneak up on you: airport transfers, tips, snacks, souvenirs, extra baggage fees, or even that extra cup of chai on the way.

Keep a small 'just in case' fund ready.

4. Book Smart, Not Cheap

Sometimes booking early or during the off-season saves money.

Sometimes last-minute deals can be great.

Always ask your agent to help you find the best options based on your budget and timing.

5. Be Flexible

If your dates or destinations are flexible, you might find better prices. Even shifting your trip by a few days or choosing a lesser-known location can bring surprising savings and joy.

"A budget is telling your money where to go instead of wondering where it went."

~ Dave Ramsey

CHAPTER 12

Packing Tips – What to Take and What to Leave Behind

Packing is one of those things everyone dreads but can't avoid. You either end up carrying too much and feel like a walking suitcase, or too little and regret leaving your favorite things behind.

Here's how to pack smart, stay light, and still be ready for anything.

1. Make a List – Yes, Seriously!

Before you start throwing clothes and gadgets into your bag, make a checklist.

Divide it into categories like:

- ❖ Clothes
- ❖ Toiletries
- ❖ Medicines
- ❖ Documents
- ❖ Gadgets
- ❖ Snacks

It saves you from forgetting your phone charger or important medicines, which can be a big headache later.

2. Choose Clothes Wisely

- ❖ Pack clothes that can mix and match easily. One jacket, two shirts, and three pants can make many combos.
- ❖ Always carry one extra pair of socks and underwear, just in case.
- ❖ Think about the weather and activities. Going to a hill station? Don't forget your warm sweater. Beach trip? Don't forget your swimwear and sunscreen.
- ❖ Roll your clothes instead of folding. It saves space and reduces wrinkles.

3. Toiletries – Keep It Simple

- Carry travel-sized bottles for shampoo, conditioner, and body wash.
- Don't forget your toothbrush, toothpaste, and any daily kincare products.
- Pack a small first-aid kit with band-aids, painkillers, and any prescription medicines.
- **Tip:** Always keep a small packet of wet wipes or tissues handy. You never know when they'll save the day!

4. Documents and Money

- Keep your ID proofs, tickets, hotel confirmations, and emergency contacts together in one folder or pouch.
- Carry a photocopy or digital copy of important documents.
- Keep some cash ready but rely mostly on cards or mobile wallets.
- **Tip:** Don't keep all your money in one place. Split it up so you're safe if something gets lost.

5. Gadgets and Accessories

- Chargers, power banks, earphones – all must-haves.
- If you plan to take pictures, bring an extra memory card or fully charge your phone.
- A small travel adapter if you're going abroad.
- Don't forget sunglasses, caps, and hats for sun protection.

6. Extras You Might Forget

- A reusable water bottle – stay hydrated!
- Snacks – some nuts or biscuits for hunger pangs during travel.
- A foldable tote bag for shopping or extra stuff you pick up.
- Comfortable walking shoes – trust me, your feet will thank you.

7. What to Leave Behind

- Heavy books or gadgets you won't use.
- Too many clothes or shoes – remember, you can usually buy stuff if really needed.
- Expensive jewelry – not worth the risk.
- Too many toiletries – hotels usually provide basics.

Final Tip:

Pack the night before your trip and double-check your list. It is better than last-minute panic and forgetting your essentials halfway through your journey.

CHAPTER 13

How to Enjoy Your Holiday Without Stress

Holidays are meant to relax, have fun, and make memories, not to get stressed out! But sometimes, even when we try to chill, little things can turn a holiday upside down.

Here's how to keep calm, enjoy every moment, and handle the unexpected like a pro.

1. Plan But Don't Over plan

It's good to have a rough plan: places you want to visit, activities you want to do, but don't schedule every single minute. Leave some space for random fun, rest, or just wandering around.

Sometimes the best holiday moments happen when you least expect them!

2. Keep Your Expectations Realistic

No trip is 100% perfect. Flights get delayed, weather can change, hotels may have issues. It happens!

Instead of panicking, go with the flow and focus on what you can enjoy. Remember, a little hiccup won't ruin your whole holiday.

3. Stay Connected but Don't Overdo It

Check in with family and friends so they know you're safe, but avoid spending all your time on your phone or social media. Enjoy the moment instead!

Put your phone away sometimes and just soak in the experience.

4. Use Local Apps and Tech to Your Advantage

Download useful local apps for transport, food delivery, or sightseeing. For example:

- Local metro or train apps for easy travel
- Taxi or cab apps like Ola or Uber where available
- Food delivery apps for late-night cravings
- Currency converter apps to avoid confusion
- Maps and translation apps

These make your travel smoother and save time.

5. Carry Some Emergency Cash

Always keep a small amount of local currency handy for places that don't accept cards or apps. Just enough for quick buys, taxis, or tips.

6. Stay Hydrated and Take Breaks

Traveling can be tiring. Drink water often and rest when you feel tired. It keeps your energy up and mood positive.

7. Ask Locals for Tips

Locals usually know the best places to eat, visit, or shop. Often these are cheaper and more authentic than tourist spots. Don't hesitate to ask.

8. Pack a Small Emergency Kit

Band-aids, medicines, hand sanitizer, wet wipes – little things that can save a big hassle.

Remember: Holidays are about enjoying, learning, and making memories. Travel light, stress less, and **smile more. That's the real magic of a great trip.**

CHAPTER 14

The Travel Checklist – What You Must Not Forget

Traveling is exciting, but it can quickly turn stressful if you miss out on the basics or overlook important little things that make all the difference. From packing smart to arranging special needs, having a checklist saves you from last-minute panic.

Here's what I always tell my clients, and trust me, these come from years of experience dealing with all kinds of travelers and their unique demands.

Pack Smart, Pack Light

- **Clothes for all weather conditions,** because you never know when a surprise rain or chilly evening hits.
- **Comfortable shoes,** no one enjoys a holiday hobbling around with sore feet.
- **Chargers, power banks, and adapters,** don't let your phone die when you need it most.
- **Basic medicines** for headache, upset stomach, or motion sickness. Better safe than sorry.
- **Important documents** such as ID cards, passports, tickets, and insurance papers. Keep copies too, just in case.

Arrange Special Needs Early

Travel isn't one-size-fits-all, and some requests need advance planning. For example:

- **Fresh cow milk for the baby.** Yes, some parents prefer this over formula or packaged milk. I always make sure to arrange it beforehand, no last-minute hassle.
- **Babysitter? Not always needed.** Sometimes parents want to keep things simple and handle their little ones personally, especially during holidays.
- **Special dietary needs,** such as veg, non-veg, gluten-free, or allergy-friendly meals. Always inform the hotel or restaurant in advance.
- **Transportation aids** such as wheelchairs, car seats for kids, or extra luggage space.

Don't Forget These Little Extras

- **Travel pillows and eye masks** for long journeys help you rest better on flights or road trips.
- **A small backpack** or sling bag for day trips is handy for carrying water, snacks, and souvenirs.
- **Camera or phone** with enough storage. Memories deserve good snaps!
- **Local currency,** carry some cash because not everywhere accepts cards.
- **Travel insurance** is a must because peace of mind is priceless and emergencies don't knock.

Pro Tip: Always Confirm Special Requests

Whenever you book a hotel or transportation, double-check your special requests a few days before your trip. A quick call or message can save you from surprises like no fresh milk, no crib, or no vegetarian food on arrival.

CHAPTER 15

Local Apps, Online Money Tricks & Travel Hacks Nobody Tells You

Alright, let's get real. Traveling can be a bit of a headache if you don't know the local ropes. Everyone talks about the big stuff: flights, hotels, and sightseeing. But the small, little things? That's where most of us get stuck. So here's the lowdown on all those small hacks that'll make your trip smoother than butter on toast.

1. Download Local Apps Before You Go

This one's a no-brainer, but you'd be surprised how many people forget it. Every city has its own apps for metros, buses, taxis, food delivery, and even local events.

- ❖ Going to Delhi? Get the Delhi Metro app for live train updates.
- ❖ Mumbai? The best bus and local train info apps are a must.
- ❖ International? Find out what the local Uber/Lyft or Ola equivalent is and download it in advance.

Trust me, it saves a ton of waiting and standing in queues.

2. Online Money Transactions: Be Ready

Cash is still king in many places, but apps like Google Pay, PhonePe, Paytm (for India), or international ones like Revolut, Wise, or PayPal can be lifesavers.

- ❖ Top up your phone wallet before you land.
- ❖ Keep a small amount of local currency for tiny stalls and local chaiwalas who don't take cards or apps.
- ❖ Always have a backup card in case one gets blocked or doesn't work.

3. Hacking the Local Metro and Transport

Metro stations can get overwhelming: multiple lines, long queues, ticket machines that don't work, and people rushing around like crazy.

- ❖ Always check if there's a smart card you can buy. It's usually cheaper and saves you from standing in ticket lines every day.
- ❖ For metro apps, check if they have a route planner. It'll tell you the fastest way with minimum transfers.
- ❖ And yes, there's always that one uncle or aunty who loves to give unsolicited advice on metro etiquette. Ignore them and enjoy your ride!

4. Little Tips That Make a Big Difference

- ❖ Always carry a portable phone charger. Nothing worse than a dead phone when you're lost in a new city.
- ❖ Ask locals about hidden cheap food spots. Those tiny roadside dhabas or cafes usually serve the best authentic dishes.
- ❖ Avoid using roaming data. Get a local SIM card if your trip is longer than 3 days. It's cheaper and faster.
- ❖ When taking a cab, check the meter or agree on the fare beforehand to avoid surprises.
- ❖ Download offline maps. Google Maps lets you download city maps so you can navigate without the internet.

5. Metro Etiquette and Tips

- Stand on the right side of the escalator, walk on the left (especially in India).
- Let passengers get off the train before you board.
- Avoid eating or talking loudly on the metro. It's common courtesy.
- Ladies-only coaches exist on many metros. Use them if you want a safer, quieter ride.

6. The Tiny Extras That Matter

- Keep a small ziplock bag for coins and small receipts. It keeps your pockets clean and prevents losing small change.
- Carry a foldable water bottle. It saves money and the environment.
- Always have a photocopy or digital copy of your important documents, just in case.

Bonus: International Travel Tips

- **Currency Exchange:** Don't exchange all your money at the airport, they usually give bad rates. Try to find local currency exchange shops in the city or withdraw from an ATM. Watch out for fees.
- **SIM Cards and WiFi:** Buy a local SIM card once you land or rent a pocket WiFi device if you'll be moving around a lot.
- **Plug Adapters:** Different countries have different plug types and voltages. Carry a universal adapter so you're not stuck charging your phone with weird plugs.

- **Tipping Culture:** Tipping rules vary a lot. Some countries expect it, others don't. Do a quick Google search on the tipping etiquette to avoid awkward moments.
- **Language Help:** Download a language translator app like Google Translate and offline language packs. It's a lifesaver for menus, signs, or asking for directions.
- **Local Emergency Numbers:** Know the local numbers for police, ambulance, and fire. They vary from country to country.
- **Dress Codes:** Some religious and cultural sites expect modest dressing, long sleeves, scarves, etc. Check in advance.
- **Travel Insurance:** Always get travel insurance. It's one of those things you hope you never need but really don't want to be without if something goes wrong.
- **Cultural Norms:** Do a quick read-up on local customs and taboos. What's normal in one country can be offensive in another.
- **Public Transport Cards:** Many cities have travel cards like London's Oyster card or Tokyo's Suica card. Buy these for cheaper rides and faster boarding.

So yeah, no one talks about these tiny little hacks, but trust me, they make the difference between a frustrating trip and a smooth, fun adventure. Remember, ***traveling isn't just about where you go. It's about how easy and comfortable you make it for yourself.***

Pack these tips in your travel bag, and you'll be ready for anything that comes your way!

Manisha Holidays: The Legacy Continues

At Manisha Holidays, every journey is part of a larger story, one that began over 20 years ago and continues to grow with every traveler we serve.

We don't just plan holidays; we build legacies that last beyond the suitcase and the calendar.

Mrs. Manisha's vision is clear: to nurture a travel community where trust, care, and heartfelt experiences are passed down to future generations. Because travel is more than destinations. It's memories shared, bonds strengthened, and cultures embraced with open arms.

Looking ahead, we're excited to expand our footprint. From the lush greens of our Corbett resort to new experiences designed to reconnect you with nature and yourself, the future is bright and meaningful.

We're also building **exclusive travel clubs** where like-minded explorers can come together to share stories, tips, and adventures because the joy of travel multiplies when shared.

The road to 2040 is paved with innovation, yes, but with a foundation rooted firmly in our core values: **Atithi Devo Bhava,** authenticity, and personalized care.

We invite you to be part of this journey, not just as guests, but as family.

Together, let's keep the spirit of travel alive, not just for today, but for generations to come.

Ashok Pandey
★★★★★ 12 weeks ago

Wow!!!Our Thailand trip was so awesome.. Thanks to Manisha Holiday and to all supporting members who coordinated our trip and we are grateful to all for making our trip so memorable. 🙏 Thanks from the bottom of my heart ❤️.

Neera Mittal
★★★★★ 8 weeks ago

The trip was fantastic . Everything was very well planned and uneventful .MANISHA HOLIDAYS IS THE ONLY ONE WHICH IS TO BE CREDITED FOR THIS TOUR .THEY HAVE DESIGNED THE TOUR VERY BEAUTIFULLY AND ECONOMICALLY .

Shubham Pandey
★★★★★ 11 weeks ago

We had an unforgettable trip to Thailand with Manisha Holidays. From 22nd to 29th August, every day was beautifully planned and filled with memorable experiences. We started with the Alcazar Show in Pattaya, followed by the Coral Island Tour. On the way to Bangkok, we enjoyed Safari World and later explored the city tour, shopping, and the Chao Phraya River Cruise. In Phuket, highlights included the Fantasea Show, Phi Phi Island Tour, Tiger Kingdom, and the Dolphin Show. Everything was organized seamlessly, and we truly appreciate Manisha Holidays for making our journey so special and hassle-free.Thank you so much for making our trip memorable.

Abu Nadeem
★★★★★ 15 weeks ago

Our recent trip to Malaysia was excellently organised by Manisha groups, our stay was at Ramada suites which is really a good place for tourist to stay as most of things including good food and famous markets like China Town, Berjaya Times Square are near by , on second day we went to Genting for one day but I recommend that Genting tour should be of 2 days one day for indoor theme park and another day for outdoor theme park because both the parks cannot be covered in a single day , lots of games and adventurous activity are there to enjoy then we had a trip of Putrajaya. On 3rd day we went to Sunway Lagoon , its a water park with lots of sports activity and there is also a natural wild life habitat , total 7 parks or area are there which cannot be covered in a single , there is toy train use that train , worth to mention there is a large wooden bridge probably largest wooden bridge in world as they r mentioning, Malaca trip is not advisable if u r not interested in History, Finally u can plan day trip with tour packaged which usually ends at around 5 Pm then take rest at ur room for 2-3 hrs and then visit near by market each on every day which is at walkable distance, many more to write but I think its enough to plan ur trip.

Kamla Joshi
★★★★★ 19 weeks ago

Thanks Manisha mam for everything you did to ensure we had the best vacation in Vietnam. Excellent service , prompt responses to any queries and everything was sorted for us. We always book our holidays through this company and will continue to do so.

Dakshata Vats
★★★★★ 21 weeks ago

Thank you, Manisha, for the excellent service during our trip to Malaysia. Everything was well-organized, and your guidance made the experience smooth and memorable. Malaysia is a beautiful country with rich culture, friendly people, and amazing food – we truly enjoyed every moment!

Neelesh Mittal
★★★★☆ 21 weeks ago

It was a wonderful and hassle free experience with Manisha holidays. I strongly recommend.

ashim rai
★★★★★ 21 weeks ago

I used the services of Manisha Holidays for my B-1 US visa to travel for a conference. They were very professional and helpful (especially Ms Shikha Juneja). They promptly and patiently answered all my queries and doubts. Due to their untiring efforts, I managed to secure a B-1 visa appointment even though I had applied through them with only a month left for my conference. I would highly recommend the services of Manisha holidays !!

Let's Keep the Journey Going

Thank you for giving your valuable time to read this book. It means a lot. 🙏

From short breaks to bucket-list journeys, you're now equipped with everything it takes to plan a holiday that truly reflects you.

Now you have two choices:

1. You can use this book as your guide and explore on your own.

Or

2. If you'd like me to walk beside you to help, advise, or answer any questions, you can easily schedule a 1-2-1 meeting with me.

Whether it's a quick query or full trip planning, I'm here.

And booking with **Manisha Holidays** is just as simple:

📞 Call or WhatsApp: +91-9917227444

✉ Email: Holidaysamit@hotmail.com | info@manishaholidays.com

🌐 Website: www.manishaholidays.com

Let's make your next holiday easy, joyful, and truly yours.

Warm regards,

Amit Singh